D0566385

T1-AYF-641

The World of Work

Choosing a Career in the Restaurant Industry

A career in the restaurant industry allows you to be creative and earn a good income.

The World of Work

Choosing a Career in the Restaurant Industry

Eileen Beal

THE ROSEN PUBLISHING GROUP, INC.
NEW YORK

Published in 1997, 1999 by The Rosen Publishing Group, Inc.
29 East 21st Street, New York, NY 10010

Revised Edition 1999

Library of Congress Cataloging-in-Publication Data

Beal, Eileen.
Choosing a career in the restaurant industry / Eileen Beal.
p. cm.—(The world of work)
Includes bibliographical references and index.
Summary: Introduces various career opportunities in the restaurant industry, from wait staff to managers to owners.
ISBN 0-8239-3002-5
1. Food service—Vocational guidance—Juvenile literature. [Restaurants—vocational guidance.] I. Title. II. Series: World of work (New York, NY)
TCX911.3.V62B43 1997
647.95'023—dc20 96-9451
CIP
AC

Manufactured in the United States of America

Contents

More and more Americans are dining outside of their homes.

We All Need to Eat

1

"Cooking with my mom has always been my favorite thing to do," says fourteen-year-old Janine. "I would love a job that would pay me to cook. What are my options?"

For sixteen-year-old Matt, working with people is his number one priority. "Everyone always says that I'm a really patient and friendly person. What kinds of professions will allow me to interact with different types of people?"

Dexter has worked in his uncle's office supply store for the past two summers. His responsibilities included checking equipment and even hiring other employees. "I've always been good with technical equipment. Also, I like being organized, especially when it comes to keeping track of supplies and materials. What other kinds of jobs require these skills?"

The answer to all three questions? The *restaurant industry*. The restaurant industry, which is part of the larger *food service industry*, includes both expensive restaurants and fast-food chains. Every kind of eating establishment, from upscale restaurants to school cafeterias to fast-food places, is a part of the food services industry. In this book we mainly discuss the restaurant industry. The information presented here, however, can also apply to jobs in other areas of the food service industry.

"I wanted a job with flexibility where I could explore many different kinds of tasks and move up the career ladder quickly," says Carlos. He noticed that new workers at a local restaurant were able to move up to better positions within a year. Also, some worked day shifts, others worked night shifts, and some worked both. "After ten months as a waiter at the restaurant, I have already learned how to prepare and serve food, and the manager has offered to teach me about her responsibilities too."

Carlos points out many of the positive parts of his job, but a career in the restaurant industry can have a negative side as well. The hours can be long, and it can be difficult to plan around irregular work schedules. Entry-level pay is not high. The work is often physically demanding, especially when you have to be on your feet. And you serve people who can be hard to please.

Still, the payoff is worthwhile. In the restaurant business you can go as far up the career ladder as your creativity, drive, and ambition will carry you.

Everyone Needs to Eat

Why is the career outlook so good for the restaurant industry?

Because everyone eats. And today more Americans are eating out than ever before. That makes for a booming industry. Statistics show:

- More than 25 percent of the nation's retail businesses are eating or drinking establishments.
- The food service industry—with 9.4 million employees—is the leading retail employer in the nation.
- Almost half of the adult population eats at least one meal a day in a restaurant.

There are restaurants to fit everybody's tastes.

- Americans spend $.44 of every food dollar on food that is eaten away from home.
- By the year 2000, more than half of the meals Americans eat will be prepared outside the home.

Why are people dining out more?

Many times people don't have time to shop for food, or prepare it, or eat it at home.

Also, the number and kinds of restaurants have grown. Restaurants, fast-food places, delis, diners, coffee shops, cafeterias, and bistros are everywhere. Grocery stores' prepared-food shops and catering businesses are not part of the food service industry, but they offer the two things restaurants specialize in: service and prepared food.

The number of full-service restaurants is growing. The number of fast-food places is declining somewhat. This is good news for people considering a career in the restaurant industry. Full-service restaurants employ more people. They offer entry-level employees a wider variety of job choices. And their employees tend to stay longer in their jobs.

The restaurant industry as a whole has begun to offer more full-time employment, higher wages, better benefits, and more training. It has also started to actively recruit more women and minorities.

Although better working conditions and benefits have attracted more people to the restaurant industry, it can be difficult to fill restaurant jobs. This is especially true in smaller towns, says Tim Michitsch, head of the Culinary Arts Program at the Joint Vocational School in Lorain County, Ohio.

"I get calls all the time that I can't fill. There is a major shortage of employees in the restaurant industry," he says. "It's a shortage in all three areas—back-of-the-house, front-of-the-house, and management."

While *salary*, or how much money a person earns, should definitely be a factor in whether to take a job in one restaurant over another, it should not be the deciding factor.

"You earn two things from a job, money and experience," explains Jan Delucia, the manager of the Hospitality Management Program at Cuyahoga County Community College in Cleveland, Ohio. "With money, you buy what you want," she adds. "With the experience—the new skills, insights, abilities—you get from a job, you move up the career ladder."

Questions to Ask Yourself

The restaurant industry is growing quickly. It offers a nontraditional work environment. And it has many opportunities for advancement. 1) Do you like the idea of working hours that are different from 9 A.M. to 5 P.M.? Why? 2) What type of restaurant would you like to work in?

The Kitchen: Back of the House

2

Misty Turner is nineteen years old. She is head line cook at the Sandusky Yacht Club in Sandusky, Ohio. Since she is on the evening shift, she sleeps until noon and gets to work by 3 P.M.

After talking with the chef about the evening's specials, she stocks her station and sets up for the evening. That means doing everything from cutting and frying onions and mushrooms, to pulling steaks and burger patties from the freezer, to making sure she has enough parsley to add to her plates.

The evening rush begins around 4:30 P.M. "Things are hectic from 5:30 till 9:30 because I'm working both the grill and the stove," she explains. "On an average night I'll get between 100 and 200 orders."

Around 10 P.M., Misty begins cleaning the grill and stove, wrapping unused food, and sweeping and mopping the floor. "I really hate clean-up—especially mopping the floor," admits Misty, "but it's part of the job."

A prep cook gets foods ready. He may crack hundreds of eggs open for breakfast, and chop hundreds of carrots and other vegetables for dinner.

Restaurants are team organizations. To function, the *back-of-the-house* people (kitchen), *front-of-the-house* people (dining room), and *over-the-house* people (managers) must work together. But it's what goes on in the restaurant's kitchen that makes or breaks a restaurant.

The person heading up the kitchen staff is the *executive chef* or *head cook*. He is called a head cook if the restaurant is small and the menu is simple. She is called an executive chef if the restaurant's aim is to serve unique, gourmet-style meals.

Executive chefs or head cooks are responsible for all activities in their kitchens. They plan menus and help set menu prices, decide on portion sizes and servings, order supplies, make sure all equipment is in working order, train employees, and "innovate."

Innovate has different meanings. Sometimes it means creating new menu items using the latest diet and health guidelines. At other times it means changing the menu because of seasonal produce or good buys. Always it means finding newer, better, and safer ways to complete kitchen tasks.

The Brigade

No cook or chef works alone. He or she works with a team called a brigade. Usually they work in a small, cramped space, so work is divided up into *stations*. Each station is overseen by the following staff members:

The *sous chef* or *assistant chef* oversees the preparation of soups, sauces, and special menu items. He or she is usually in charge during shifts when the chef is not present.

The *pastry chef/baker* prepares baked goods, including breads and dessert items.

The *garde manger* or *salad person* is considered the pantry supervisor in large kitchens. He or she washes and cuts fruits and vegetables used in salads or other dishes.

A *short order cook* (also *line cook*, *fry cook*, or *broiler cook*) prepares foods in small restaurants and fast-food places.

The *prep cook* or *kitchen assistant* (also *cook's helper*) prepares foods to be cooked. He or she lays out the tools and equipment needed by the chef and assistant chef. He or she also cleans work areas.

The *dishwasher* washes dining room china and silver and kitchen pots and pans. This person is often responsible for kitchen clean-up, including sweeping and mopping the floor.

Pastry chefs often work through the night to make the pastries that people enjoy first-thing in the morning.

The *kitchen manager* or *kitchen supervisor* coordinates work schedules and food-related events. He or she orders food and supplies.

The *corporate chef* is usually not a working chef, but rather one who manages the kitchens in hotels or restaurants.

A *menu planner* or *menu consultant* works with the chef to create new menu items and recipes. This person often has a college degree in nutrition and is employed on a part-time or contract basis.

There are no formal requirements for most of the jobs in a kitchen. But back-of-the-house jobs do require a great deal of firsthand knowledge and experience. Much of it can be gained at home, in high school vocational education programs, two-year certificate programs at community colleges or technical colleges, or in four-year programs at colleges or universities. It can also be gained at private culinary schools, such as the highly respected Culinary Institute of America and Johnson and Wales University.

Most back-of-the house employees gain their initial experience by taking a job in a kitchen during the summer or on weekends. As dishwashers, prep cooks, or salad preparers they observe, learn, and put their new skills to use—and take that first step up the career ladder.

Once on the career ladder, back-of-the-house employees tend to shift around in various positions as they move up. Job-hopping is expected, says Michitsch.

"That way," he explains, "you are learning a lot of things—techniques, cooking and preparation styles, recipes—from a number of different people and in different situations.

"That," he adds, "just makes you better at the job."

Back-of-the-house pay still begins at minimum wage. Salaries vary according to job title and experience. A line cook at a small restaurant may earn roughly $23,000 per year, while an experienced chef can make up to $150,000 per year. In extremely prestigious restaurants, executive chefs can earn over $200,000 per year.

Questions to Ask Yourself

There are many back-of-the-house jobs. 1) Does this area of the restaurant industry interest you? 2) Which job appeals to you the most? 3) How can you gain experience in the kitchen?

3

Front of the House: It's Not Just Meet and Greet

Thirty-year-old Jay Johnson has been supporting himself as a waiter since 1984. For the last two years, he has worked the lunch shift at 12th and Porter, a well-known restaurant in Nashville, Tennessee.

He gets up between 8 and 9 A.M. and is at work by 10:15 A.M. The restaurant does not require servers to wear uniforms, so he wears a nice shirt, nice slacks, and a tie.

When he arrives at work, he and the other servers begin prepping for lunch. They make sure the tables are properly set, the coffee and tea are brewing, and the salad dressings are made. Since Jay likes to serve healthy dishes, he always prepares a low-fat dressing. It has become a popular item.

At 11:30 A.M., the restaurant opens, and by noon it is crowded. From then until 1:30 P.M., Jay is moving constantly. He puts in orders to the kitchen, serves food, checks how things are going at each table, delivers

A waiter must make sure all of his tables are ready before the dining room opens.

checks, and clears and sets tables. "It's really crazy," says Jay.

By 1:30 or 2 P.M., Jay can begin closing down his station. "Usually that's four to six tables," he says, "but on Wednesdays and Fridays it can go up to ten or twelve."

When his station is closed, he checks out with the hostess. Checking out means paying his bar and meal charges, collecting tips that were included in credit card payments, and checking the schedule for the next day.

Jay doesn't see himself being a waiter for the rest of his life, but it's definitely the right job for him now.

"I can set my own hours, and in a twenty to twenty-five hour work week I make as much as most people make in a forty-hour work week," he says. "And I can work anywhere."

When people dine out, they purchase two products: food and service. The back-of-the-house people provide the food. The front-of-the-house employees deliver the service.

Working up front—where it's often spacious and nicely decorated—is just as demanding as working in the kitchen. But the demands are different.

Front-of-the-house employees, just like those in the kitchen, are team players. All employees from any kind of restaurant have these traits in common:

- They are organized, and they are good with math. They must be able to serve several customers at one time, remember what each person ordered, and add up the bill correctly.
- They are outgoing, and they like people.
- They handle the stress of doing several tasks at once. These tasks may include taking food orders, delivering meals, adding up guest checks, and clearing tables.

A server's attitude often plays a part in how much a customer enjoys his or her experience in the restaurant.

- They are physically strong. They are on their feet for long periods of time. They lift heavy things—everything from trays of hot food to boxes of liquor. They do a lot of bending and stretching.
- They are dependable. They are depended on to work efficiently, especially during rush hours. Restaurant rush hours come three times a day—6:30–9 A.M., 11:30 A.M.–1:30 P.M., and 5–8 P.M.

The Front-of-the-House People

Servers (*waiters* and *waitresses*) are a restaurant's most visible employees. They take orders and relay them to the kitchen. They serve food and beverages, and check with customers to make sure everything is all right. They also keep water glasses and coffee cups filled, and fill out checks. In small restaurants, they may also set and clear tables and replace supplies. In expensive restaurants, they advise patrons about food and wine and prepare some items, such as salads or desserts, at the table. Servers often use computers to place food and drink orders and record customers' payments.

Servers usually work in *shifts*. A shift is a period of time during which a person works. In the restaurant industry, shifts focus around meal times: breakfast, lunch, and dinner. Servers may work a breakfast shift, lunch shift, or dinner shift. Or they may work *split shifts*. A split shift means that a server works two shifts, with a long break in between. For instance, a server may work the lunch shift from 11:30 A.M. to 2 P.M. Then he may relax, have lunch himself, or even go home until the dinner shift begins at 4:30 P.M.

Servers move up the career ladder two ways. In small or mid-size restaurants, they move up to *head waiter* or *dining room manager* positions.

The head waiter or dining room manager is in charge of all the other servers. She trains all new wait staff. She makes sure everyone is at his shift on time, in uniform, and ready to work. She may make up the weekly schedule. She makes sure that all the details involved in serving and clearing meals are taken care of. For example, she may check to see that the wait station shelves are stocked with enough coffee and tea. She may also make sure that there are plenty of tablecloths, napkins, silverware, and water glasses available to quickly reset a table after the customers leave. The head waiter or dining room manager may also be responsible for closing out the cash register and balancing all the receipts for the night against the money in the register.

In larger or fancier restaurants, a server may move up to become the *wait captain* or *maitre d'*. The wait captain or maitre d' oversees the entire dining room during a shift. He makes sure that all customers are served efficiently and to their satisfaction. He may seat special customers, solve a problem between two servers, or open a bottle of champagne for a couple celebrating their engagement. A wait captain or maitre d' must always have everything under control. He must never lose his temper, even when a customer is being unreasonable. And he must remember that the customer is always right. It's a tough job. But many people feel that the increased wages and respect are worth it.

Bartenders are also very visible front-of-the-house employees. In many areas, they must be twenty-one years old to serve liquor, but age twenty-five seems to be the industry standard. A bartender must know about beers, wines, and mixed drinks. They serve drinks at the bar, are in charge of the cash register, and clean the bar, glasses, and equipment. When the bar is connected to a restaurant, the bartender fills servers' orders too. They may also be responsible for ordering and maintaining liquor and bar supplies.

Night work, weekend work, and holiday work are common for all front-of-the-house employees, especially bartenders.

Busers or *dining room attendants* clear and set tables, carry dirty dishes to the kitchen area, clean up spilled food and broken dishes, and free up servers to work directly with customers. They may also help servers carry trays or prepare food at customers' tables. This experience helps them gain the

As a member of the wait staff in a hotel, you may be responsible for room service deliveries.

A Tip About Tips

A server's base pay is low. Tips, which can make up as much as 50 to 80 percent of a server's take home pay, make up the difference in earnings.

The federal government states that tips are income. This means that servers must pay income tax and Social Security and Medicare taxes on the tips they receive.

Servers who earn more than $20 a month in tips must report them to their employer in writing. The report, usually on a standard form, is due by the tenth of each month. It includes the employee's name, address, and social security number.

Most servers keep a daily record of tips, however, just in case the federal government wants to see a record of tips earned.

knowledge and skills needed to become servers.

The *host* or *hostess* schedules reservations, greets people as they enter the restaurant, and assigns and guides them to a table. He or she may also give menus and explain the restaurant's meal specials to customers. If problems arise, they listen to customer complaints and try to solve the situation. They take payments from servers or from diners as they leave the restaurant. At the end of their shift, they total and record all guest checks and organize the cash drawer for the next shift or the next day.

Many hosts and hostesses are former servers who are working their way up the ladder into management positions.

Most entry-level servers earn between $2.50 and $3.75 an hour in wages. The rest of their pay—which can average out to between $8 and $15 per hour—is in tips. A *tip* is a sum of money given by a customer to a server for good service.

All other entry-level front-of-the-house employees can expect to earn minimum wage. Those with more experience or who begin a job in an expensive restaurant will probably earn more than minimum wage.

Questions to Ask Yourself

You must enjoy working with and serving people to work at the front of the house.
1) Do you like working with people?
2) Would you prefer to work in a fancy restaurant or in a casual, more relaxed restaurant?

Over the House: Managing or Owning a Restaurant

4

Thirty-four-year-old Dave Garner started out in the restaurant business as a cook. He was nineteen years old and had no experience. As he learned to cook, he also learned the restaurant business. He enrolled in the Hospitality Management Program at Johnson County Community College in Overland Park, Kansas.

Now the general manager at Romano's Macaroni Grill in Overland Park, Dave begins his workday at 10 A.M. The kitchen is his first stop. "To do a quality check," he says. Then he goes to his office to review the prior day's sales, return phone calls, and take care of paperwork.

By 11:15 A.M., he has met with his staff. He also completes an overall check of the restaurant. He examines table settings, music level, bathroom cleanliness, and more. Then he talks with servers about the day's specials "and whatever else needs to be talked about."

At 11:30 A.M., the lunch rush begins. Dave helps out where he is needed. He seats guests and helps servers deliver orders and dining room attendants clear tables. He also checks the look of the dishes and the portion size and temperature of the food to maintain the quality of what they serve.

Around 2 P.M., Dave eats. "It's not a real lunch," he says, "just a refueling stop."

Afterwards, he meets with the restaurant's chef to discuss the evening's specials, his assistants to discuss problems that came up during lunch, and salespeople.

When new employees start, he explains the restaurant's policies, procedures, and standards to them. "It's really important that employees understand our procedures. We are a bit different from other family restaurants," he states. "Our servers sing opera songs and clap when someone drops a tray."

During the dinner rush, which begins at 4:30 P.M., he helps out where he is needed and is on the go until about 9 P.M.

By 9:30 or 10 P.M., Dave heads for home, where he dines with his wife and works on his computer. He is in bed by midnight.

Dave works a long day, but he loves his job. The pay is "very good," he says, and the work isn't as hard as it sounds.

"That," he brags, "is because I've got very good assistants."

Over the House People

The term "over–the–house" refers to the people who *manage* a restaurant. They hire staff, decide wages, order food and beverages, and make sure the restaurant makes money.

The *general manager* (GM) has two jobs: to make certain that the restaurant runs smoothly and that it makes a profit. Except in very small, owner-operated restaurants, the general manager can't do these jobs alone. Most restaurants have several different kind of managers. In a large restaurant, especially a chain or hotel/resort restaurant, the general manager oversees the management team. In a small restaurant, this person manages the staff, oversees food and beverage purchases, handles advertising and marketing, and may act as host/hostess and cashier.

The *assistant manager*, *trainee-manager*, or *night manager* assists the general manager in overseeing dining room and kitchen service. He or she also assumes night and holiday management duties.

Catering managers make sure that events such as weddings or luncheons go smoothly.

The *food and beverage manager* is responsible for all food and beverage operations, including liquor sales and catering.

The *purchasing manager* or *purchasing agent* meets with salespeople, purchases goods and coordinates their delivery, and attends equipment and product demonstrations.

The *floor manager* or *floor supervisor* supervises employees and coordinates food service in restaurants with more than one dining area. These restaurants are typically found in large hotels, resorts, and on cruise ships.

The *catering manager* is usually found in large hotels and institutions, such as conference and convention centers. He or she is responsible for all aspects of the catering operations. Duties may include scheduling an event, staffing it, and sending out the final bill.

The *personnel manager* supervises hiring, training, and management of employees. In smaller establishments, this person may also handle the employee benefits program.

The *district* or *regional manager* oversees the management of several eating establishments, for example, fast-food places or restaurants belonging to the same chain.

Managers bring two skills to their job: people and business skills. People skills include tact, patience, leadership ability, and the ability to communicate. These skills may come naturally, but the business skills are usually learned. In the past, managers could pick up business skills as they worked their way up the career ladder. Today, however, management jobs are more specialized. To get an entry-level management job in an eating establishment, you *must* have hospitality training from a two- or four-year school.

Associate of arts (A.A./two-year) and bachelor's degree (B.A. or B.S./four-year) hospitality management programs feature classes in the following subjects:

- food service-related topics in accounting, business law, management, and personnel
- food planning, preparation, and nutrition
- public relations and marketing
- sanitation, maintenance, and housekeeping

And education doesn't stop with school. Although today's newly hired management employees always have previous experience and a degree, they still spend time in company education programs.

"That is so [they] understand the policies and philosophy of the company," explains Dave. He spent thirteen weeks in Macaroni Grill's corporate training program, even though he had a restaurant-related college degree and had owned his own restaurant.

In management, advancement is almost always through a job change. Managers gain more pay and responsibility by moving to larger restaurants, or into higher management positions within the same company, or they jump into ownership.

Ownership

Restaurant ownership is the ultimate dream of many managers. It is a dream, however, that many managers, including Dave, have tried and then put aside.

Why? "Because ownership is a twenty-four-hour-a-day, seven-days-a-week job," says Dave. And few (only one in five) owner-operated restaurants survive more than three years. This includes the restaurants that get rave reviews from customers and high ratings in restaurant guides.

Most managers who want their own restaurant open a franchise restaurant.

Owning your own restaurant requires a lot of hard work and long days.

Opening a franchise restaurant—from a Burger King fast-food place to a full-service restaurant, such as Applebee's Neighborhood Grill and Bar—is difficult. Franchise applicants go through a long and thorough screening process. And it is costly. Successful applicants pay a fee to open the restaurant. Then they make ongoing payments to the franchise corporation. The franchise corporation encourages franchise owners to run their establishments their own way. However, the corporation insists that each franchise conform to strict standards and guidelines.

Many people decide to open a restaurant that’s part of a franchise or chain.

Still, for those managers who open franchises, it fulfills the dream of owning a restaurant.

Income

Earnings for entry-level positions vary greatly. Fast-food restaurants are the easiest places to break into food service management. However, they usually pay managers less than a full-service restaurant would. A manager in a fast-food restaurant typically earns $25,000 per year. In full-service restaurants, new managers can expect to make between $30,000 and $33,000. Managers working in commercial and institutional settings, such as colleges and hospitals, earn between $26,000 and $33,000 per year. Managers often receive *bonuses* of between $1,000 and $8,000 in addition to their salaries.

Questions to Ask Yourself

Managing or owning a restaurant is a huge responsibility. 1) What are your goals for a career in the restaurant industry? Do they include one day becoming a manager or owner? 2) How can you learn about the responsibilities involved in being a manager or owner?

A good way to get into the restaurant industry is by working as a dishwasher.

Find Out for Yourself 5

There are many ways to learn about the restaurant industry. Two of them that we will discuss in this chapter are getting a job at a restaurant and talking to someone who works in the industry in an informational interview.

Getting a Job

The most obvious way to try out a food service career is to get a job in a restaurant's kitchen or dining room. More entry-level jobs are available during the summer than the rest of the year. There are more jobs in big cities and vacation areas, such as in or near scenic locations, amusement parks, resorts, and beaches, than in small towns and rural areas.

Many resort areas and theme parks—including Six Flags Over Texas, Cedar Point, and SeaWorld—sponsor job fairs in January and February to recruit summer employees for their restaurants, cafes, and concession stands. Though they usually do not hire people under eighteen years of age, they do hire people with no prior experience. This makes them excellent sources of entry-level restaurant jobs.

The skills required by these entry-level jobs—as servers, dining room attendants, hostesses, kitchen assistants, dishwashers—are all learned on the job. They are easily learned by observing or working with more experienced workers. While you are learning and earning money, you are also seeing if you like the work, the hours, and dealing with the public.

The best way to find a job is to go into an eating establishment you think you might want to work in and ask the owner or manager if there are any openings. Try a neighborhood family restaurant, a resort's cafe, a national park's concession stand, or a local hotel's restaurant. Go even if there are no "help wanted" signs in the window. Be sure to time your visit when the restaurant is not busy (before 11:30 A.M. or between 2 and 4 P.M.). Even if the owner or manager says there are no openings, leave your name and phone number in case there should be an opening in the near future.

The food service industry includes everything from four-star restaurants to roadside hot dog stands.

The next best way to find an entry-level job is to scan your local newspaper's want ads. Look in the "restaurant" section, and look for the terms "entry level" and "part time" in the ads.

If your school has a job bulletin board, check it out. If it doesn't, ask your school's guidance counselor for leads on job openings in local eating establishments.

And don't neglect your friends, family, or neighbors. Let them know you are looking for a restaurant job. They might know of a restaurant that is hiring.

Informational Interview

If you can't get a job in a restaurant, talk to people who are working in the food service industry.

That's what Dave Garner did when he was looking for his first job.

"I did interviews with people I knew who worked in restaurants, and people the director [of the hospitality management program he eventually enrolled in] told me about," says Dave.

During the interviews, the people he talked to discussed with him the pros and cons of working in the food service industry. They told him about the long hours. They told him about the stamina he would need. But they also told him how the industry was growing, and how "a career in a food service establishment could be a long-term income opportunity."

"Most important of all," Dave points out, "they told me—all of them—that I needed to get experience in both the back-of-the-house and front-of-the-house if I wanted to move into management . . . and that working while I went to school was a good way to get that kind of hands-on perspective."

If possible, schedule the interview at the restaurant but make sure to do it during the restaurant's slow hours.

Questions to Ask

- How long have you been a (waiter/waitress, cook, chef, host/hostess, manager)?
- How did you get this job? Did you answer a newspaper ad? Did a friend tell you about it?
- Describe an "average" day from the time you get to work in the morning until you get home at night.
- What are the working conditions like at this restaurant? Are they the same here as at the place you last worked? Are these conditions typical for the industry?
- What is the best thing about this job?
- What is the worst thing about this job?
- What are the personal skills that you brought into the (kitchen, dining room, management office) with you?
- What special skills did you realize you needed to learn to get where you are today? Where did you learn these additional skills—in school or on the job?
- Are you paid in (tips, wages, salary)?
- What is the salary range for your position?

An outgoing personality and a sense of humor are excellent qualities for someone in the restaurant industry to have.

- What kinds of benefits (health insurance, sick days, vacation days) does your employer offer? Are they the standard benefits for the industry?
- Do you know anyone else I can talk to? Can you give me their names and phone numbers?

Skills and Attitude That Spell Success

Before you think about a career in the restaurant industry, ask yourself the following questions. If you can answer most of them with a firm yes, a restaurant career may be ideal for you.

Personal Skills

Am I friendly and patient with people?
Do I have an outgoing personality?
Do I have a good sense of humor?
Am I self-confident?
Am I physically strong?
Am I neat and tidy?

Business Skills

Can I work as part of a team?
Am I organized and detail-oriented?
Do I work efficiently and effectively?
Am I good at math?
Do I communicate well?

Service Attitude

Do I like the idea of serving and helping others?
Am I bored by routine, repetitive work?
Am I interested in the business of food?

Questions to Ask Yourself

There are several ways to get information about the restaurant industry. 1) With whom can you have an informational interview? 2) What questions would you ask? 3) What skills do you need to be successful in this field?

Most front-of-the-house employees learn their skills on the job.

Opening the Door to a Restaurant Career 6

It pays to get training or education before you begin a restaurant career. In some jobs, trained workers can earn as much as $150 per week more than untrained employees.

There are no formal training programs for people who want entry-level front-of-the-house jobs. However, many high school vocational education (vo-ed) and community college culinary arts and hospitality management programs offer courses that are very useful to people who work in a restaurant's dining room. Course subjects include computers, psychology, and communications.

Most servers, dining room attendants, hosts, hostesses, and bartenders learn their jobs through on-the-job training sessions with a manager or under the watchful eye of more experienced employees. In certain establishments, especially fast-food chains, some on-the-job training is done with

There are many great culinary arts programs for future cooks or chefs.

videos. As computers become more common, interactive training programs will also be used.

Several different kinds of schools offer programs that prepare people for careers in back-of-the-house and over-the-house positions. Excellent career training programs are offered for high school juniors and seniors at city- or county-wide vocational, or vo-ed, schools.

“These programs,” notes instructor Tim Michitsch, “are a real benefit to people going into the restaurant field. They help students succeed much more quickly in post-high school programs.”

Additional programs are offered through local vocational-technical, or vo-tech, centers, junior or community colleges, private trade schools, and in the Armed Forces.

Both public and private schools are listed in the classified section of your local newspaper and in the "schools" section of your local phone book. Private school programs are much more expensive than vo-ed, vo-tech, and junior or community college programs.

The Armed Forces food service programs are extensive, and depending on the ambition of the recruit, can include training in both cooking and food service management. Training in the Armed Forces has two extra bonuses: it's free and it can usually count toward trade school or college credit.

Getting formal training isn't just a smart money move, it's a smart career move, too. Programs are specifically designed to teach entry-level-or-better skills in a relatively short period of time. They use modern equipment, and most instructors are currently working in the food service industry or have extensive food service-related experience. Programs stress hands-on training, and often have co-op programs that let students learn and earn money at the same time. They usually offer

Chefs at prestigious restaurants are expected to create meals that are both beautiful and delicious.

both day and evening classes. Courses taken at a community college can usually be transferred to a four-year college. Most programs are relatively inexpensive, and they usually help graduates find jobs once their training is completed.

These programs, especially those at vo-ed schools, vo-tech centers, and community colleges, get calls all the time from restaurants and other food service institutions that are looking for employees. They usually get more requests than they can fill.

Also, most instructors work in the local restaurant industry. They know about job openings and pass the word along to the school's job placement counselor or to the students themselves.

Finding the Best Match

Before you invest time and money in a program to prepare yourself for a career in the restaurant industry, investigate the program.

Get the school's tuition and refund policy in writing. Discuss the school's work-study program and emergency leave policy.

Find out whether the school and its program are *accredited*. Accreditation is done by agencies from the food service industry that are recognized by the U.S. Department of Education. Accreditation means that the school, its instructors, and its programs have met industry standards. It also means that the certificate, diploma, or degree it awards is recognized in the food service industry. Enrolling in an accredited school usually allows students to get loans or other financial aid from the U.S. government.

Find out about a program's student dropout rate and teacher turnover rate. A high dropout rate usually means students are dissatisfied with the program. High instructor turnover usually means there are problems with the school's programs and administration.

Check out the school's job placement department and its job placement rate. Good schools don't just list jobs on a bulletin board. They also:

- Have a full- or part-time trained job counselor on staff.
- Match graduates with jobs in which they will succeed.
- Offer job placement services to current graduates and to previous graduates too.
- Help students write résumés and obtain

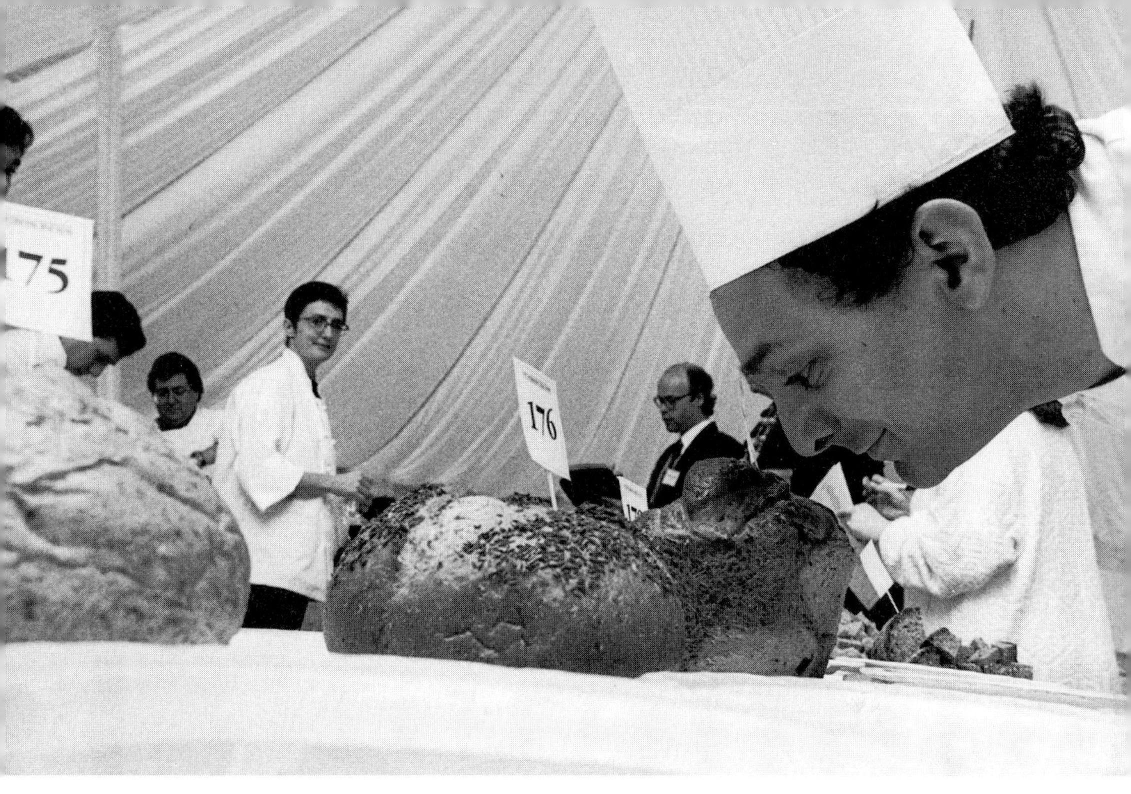

As a student in a culinary school or program, your work will be judged and graded by professionals in the field.

reference letters from instructors and previous employers.
- Help students set up and prepare for interviews.

Another important thing to do is tour the school's facilities. Look at the classrooms, the training kitchen and restaurant, and the library/resource center. This is the best way to see what the school is like and if it seems to be managed well.

Try to attend both beginner and advanced-level classes in the program you are interested in. Talk to the students. Ask them if they think the classes are too hard or too easy. Ask them how much time they spend in class and how much time they spend putting what they learn in class into practice.

Talk to instructors. Find out their training and work background. The more varied the teachers' backgrounds are, the more well-rounded the instruction will be in their classes and lab sessions.

There are many opportunities within the restaurant industry. The trick is to find the career that matches your interest, talents, skills, and goals. By now you should have an idea of what that career may be. So what are you waiting for? Go try it out!

Questions to Ask Yourself

One way to acquire some of the skills you may need in the restaurant industry is to attend a program that teaches those skills. 1) Where can you find such a program? 2) What should you find out about the program before you enroll in it? 3) What skills would you like to learn?

Glossary

accredited program Formal, school-based training program that is recognized by food service industry representatives, eating establishments, and associations as preparing students for jobs in the restaurant industry.

back-of-the-house Kitchen staff.

brigade system Organizational system in hotel or restaurant kitchens that gives each person a specific title and job.

culinary arts program Formal, hands-on educational program that trains students in kitchen skills.

food service industry Industry term for all of the types of eating establishments.

franchise The right through legal agreement given an individual or group to market a restaurant's name, goods, and services.

front-of-the-house Dining room staff.

full-service restaurant Eating establishment

that has a full menu and that serves diners at tables.

hospitality management program Formal, hands-on educational program that trains students in the skills needed to operate and manage a restaurant.

maitre d' Head server in a fine dining restaurant; usually responsible for supervising the dining room and training other servers.

innovate To introduce changes that increase productivity, efficiency, and popularity of an item or establishment.

over-the-house Management.

restaurant industry Segment of the food service industry made up solely of restaurants and fast-food establishments.

split-shift An eight-hour work day that is broken into two segments.

station In the kitchen, the area overseen by a cook or chef; in the dining room, the tables for which a server is responsible.

turnover rate Time and speed with which tables are emptied so that new diners can use them.

For More Information

Information on careers in all areas of the restaurant industry is available from:

Your high school counselor or vocational education counselor.
Your local vo-tech center or community college. (Ask about their culinary arts and hospitality management programs.)

United States Listings

American Culinary Federation
10 San Bartola Drive
St. Augustine, FL 32086-5766
(904) 824-4468
Web site: http://www.acfchefs.org

Career College Association
750 First Street NE
Washington, DC 20002-4242
(202) 336-6700
Web site: http://www.thomson.com/career/

Council on Hotel, Restaurant, and
Institutional Education
1200 17th Street NW
Washington, DC 20036
(202) 331-5990
Web site: http://www.chrie.org

Educational Foundation of the National
Restaurant Association
250 South Wacker Drive, Suite 1400
Chicago, IL 60606-5834
(800) 765-2122
Web site: http://www.edfound.org

International Association of Culinary
Professionals
304 West Liberty Street, Suite 3201
Louisville, KY 40202
(502) 581-9786

Canadian Listings:

Hotel and Restaurant Suppliers Association
2435 Guenette Street
Saint-Laurent, Quebec, Canada H4R 2E9
(800) 567-2347
Web site: http://www.afhr.com

For Further Reading

Alonzo, Roy S. *The Upstart Guide to Owning and Managing a Restaurant*. Chicago: Upstart Publishing Co., 1995.

Chmelynski, Carol Ann Caprione. *Opportunities in Restaurant Careers*. Lincolnwood, IL: VGM Career Horizons, 1998.

Dahmer, Sandra, and Kurt Kahl. *The Waiter and Waitress Training Manual*. New York: Van Nostrand Reinhold, 1995.

Education Foundation of the National Restaurant Association. *A Guide to Two-Year and Four-Year Colleges and Universities with Foodservice/Hospitality Programs*. Chicago: Education Foundation of the National Restaurant Association.

Lidz, Richard, and Linda Perrin. *Career Information Center: Hospitality and Recreation*. Vol. 8. New York: MacMillan Publishing Company, 1993.

Powers, Thomas F., and Tom Powers.

Introduction to Management in the Hospitality Industry. New York: John Wiley & Sons, 1995.

Restaurant and Institute Council on Hotels. *A Guide to College Programs in Hospitality and Tourism*. 5th ed. Restaurant and Institute Council on Hotels. New York: John Wiley & Sons, 1997.

U.S. Department of Labor, Bureau of Labor Statistics, 1994–95. *Occupational Outlook Handbook; Business and Managerial Occupations; Service Occupations*. Washington, DC: U.S. Department of Labor, Bureau of Labor Statistics, 1994–95.

Vocational Biographies (biographies covering jobs one could have in a restaurant). Sauk Center, MN: 1992–95.

Index

About the Author

Eileen Beal has an M.A. in history and museum education. She has worked as a junior and senior high school social studies teacher, an assistant editor for both magazines and newspapers, a free-lance food and restaurant critic, and a free-lance writer. Ms. Beal's works include social studies curriculum, museum exhibit wall text, and numerous articles about food, cooking, and culinary education issues.

Photo Credits: Cover, p. 24 © Cliff Hollenbeck/International Stock; p. 2 © Frank Grant/International Stock; p. 6 © F. M. Kearney/Impact Visuals; p. 10 © Shia Photo/Impact Visuals; pp. 14, 48 © Rick Gerharter/Impact Visuals; p. 17 © Gregory Edwards/International Stock; p. 21 © Jay Thomas/ International Stock; p. 27 © Mark Bolster/International Stock; p. 33 © Stan Ries/International Stock; pp. 37, 43, 46 © Bill Stanton/International Stock; p. 38 © Cindy Reiman/Impact Visuals; p. 40 © Earl Dotter/Impact Visuals; p. 51 © Jonathan E. Pite/International Stock; p. 52 © Lou Manna/ International Stock; p. 55 © Stephanie Rausser/Impact Visuals.

Design: Erin McKenna